CACTUS POEMS

Poems by FRANK ASCH   Photographs and Notes by TED LEVIN

A GULLIVER GREEN BOOK   HARCOURT BRACE & COMPANY   *San Diego   New York   London*

Library of Congress Cataloging-in-Publication Data
Asch, Frank.
Cactus poems/written by Frank Asch; photographed by Ted Levin.
p. cm.
"Gulliver Green."
Summary: Poems and photographs depict desert ecosystems
in North America.
ISBN 0-15-200676-1
1. Children's poetry, American.   [1. Deserts—Poetry.
2. American poetry.]   I. Levin, Ted, ill.   II. Title.
PS3551.S3C33   1998
811'.54—dc21   96-50351

G F E D C

Printed in Singapore

Gulliver Green® books focus on various aspects of ecology
and the environment, and a portion of the proceeds from the sale of
these books is donated to protect, preserve, and restore native forests.

FRONT COVER PHOTOS: Western screech owl peeking out of a nest cavity in a saguaro. *Green
Valley, AZ, April 1995.* Saguaros and blooming brittlebush. *Sabino Canyon, Tucson, AZ, April 1992.*
BACK COVER PHOTO: Bighorn lamb climbing on his father's back. *Arizona-Sonora Desert Museum,
Tucson, AZ, April 1995.* COPYRIGHT PAGE PHOTO: Skull of bighorn ram. *Anza-Borrego Desert State
Park, CA, April 1989.* DEDICATION PAGE PHOTO: Mound cactus flower. *Joshua Tree National Park,CA,
April 1991.* TITLE PAGE PHOTO: Alpenglow on the Panamint Mountains reflected in Badwater.
Death Valley National Park, CA, March 1991. INTRODUCTION PHOTO: Tiger rattlesnake. *Tucson
Mountains, AZ, April 1990.*

*We are grateful to the staff at the Arizona-Sonora Desert
Museum, Tucson, Arizona; to Cyrie Lang's third grade class
at Thetford Elementary School, Thetford, Vermont; and to
our editors, Liz Van Doren and Alison Hagge.*

The photographs in this book were taken with Nikon camera bodies
and lenses, ranging from 24mm to 800mm, off a Gitzo tripod. The film
used was Fuji 50 & 100, Fuji Velvia, and Kodachrome 25 & 64.
The display type was set in Herculanum.
The text type was set in Cochin and Perpetua Italic.
Color separations by United Graphic Pte Ltd.
Printed and bound by Tien Wah Press, Singapore
This book was printed on totally chlorine-free
Nymolla Matte Art paper.
Production supervision by Stanley Redfern and Ginger Boyer
Designed by Ted Levin and Camilla Filancia

To my tattoo brother, Casey
    —F. A.

To Tristan, with love—may your desert walks
be thornless
    —T. L.

INTRODUCTION

I'll never forget my first trip to the desert more than twenty-five years ago. One night, while I was hitchhiking from coast to coast, the rodeo cowboy who was giving me a lift dropped me off about one hundred miles west of Tucson, Arizona.

"Watch out for rattlesnakes," he warned. "They come out onto the road to get warm when the temperature drops. And don't go in the bushes. Those bushes are full of rattlers!" As I watched his taillights disappear into the night, all I could see was road and bushes.

It was two o'clock in the morning. Above me the Milky Way poured from horizon to horizon. But that night I couldn't appreciate the beauty of the desert. All I could think about was *snakes.*

There is a well-known rule of writing that says: You can't write what you don't know. So I knew I had to return to the desert before I wrote the poetry for this book. I had to enter as a child, touch the soul of the place, and let it speak through me.

This, I know, was an ambitious goal. But I had excellent help. My friend and collaborator, Ted Levin, is not just an accomplished nature photographer. He's also a scientist and a naturalist with many years of experience in the desert. He knows the land of cactus like he knows his own backyard.

With Ted as my guide, I was able to see the desert with fresh eyes. One day while walking toward an oasis, we came upon a diamondback rattlesnake in a mesquite bush a few feet from our path. The sudden burst of his rattle startled me. My first response was to run, but Ted encouraged me to stay and watch.

"Most snakebites happen when people attack the snakes and not the other way around," he said. "Only one in four snakebites to humans contains venom. They prefer to save it for their prey. And did you know that the Hopi people view rattlesnakes as fertility symbols? The sound of the rattle reminds them of the sound of rain on the hard-packed desert earth." After a while the snake grew quiet and slithered away.

Ted not only shared his knowledge with me, he shared his passion for the spirit of the desert. The trill of the canyon wren in the morning or the glowing eyes of pocket mice raiding our campsite at night filled him with an infectious sense of wonder and joy. Once when we were stuck in an airport for hours he said, "I know I'd feel better if I could just hold a snake."

Somewhere in our travels, I shed my fear of wild places like a rattler sheds his too-small skin. Before I left the desert, even *I* was holding snakes (gopher snakes, not rattlers).

Facts and feelings, like science and art, are often separated. But in this book you'll find them working side by side, breaking down the walls we've placed between ourselves and nature.

No poem can be a substitute for sitting on a hill amid ancient petroglyphs or watching mountain shadows creep across the desert floor. No photograph can reproduce the experience of standing next to a giant saguaro or listening to the coyote's eerie howl. But I hope this book can at least introduce you to the desert I've come to know. May it lead you to the soul of all wild places. May you walk in them and someday let them speak through you.

—FRANK ASCH

Middletown Springs, Vermont

BREAKS FREE

I just want to be
where the earth breaks free
of concrete and metal and glass,
of asphalt and plastic and gas,
where sun is king
and water is queen,
where cactus grow tall
and the air is clean.
I just want to be
where the earth breaks free
of fences and alleys and walls,
of factories and traffic and malls,
where owls sleep
in the heat of day
waiting for sunset
to hunt their prey,
where mountains rise
in seas of sand
and coyotes roam
across the land.

  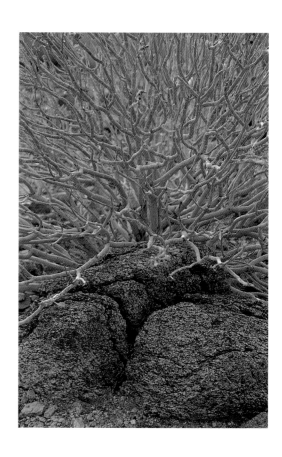

WATER SECRET

Everyone here keeps a secret.
Some sing for her.
Some sting for her.
Some make her.
Some take her.
Some grow wide and round for her.

Some grow deep and straight for her.
Some dig a hole. Some wait for her.
But everyone here keeps a secret,
a secret that helps them grow.
A wet secret, a deep secret,
a secret the sun must never know.

WATERLESS SHORES

There is no stream to draw them,
so they come to the flowers to feed.
First come the ants, bees, and moths
looking for nectar, pollen, and seed.

Then come their predators,
mantis, spider, and rat;
then predators of predators,
lizard, snake, and cat.

They come to the desert flower
to feed at its waterless shore,
where rivers of color run wild
and waterfalls of fragrance roar.

THE OLDEST

Not tall. Not pretty.
My wood has no worth.
But I *am* the oldest
living thing on earth.

When shadows are sharp
and leaves hard to keep,
my roots stay safe and wet
so far, so way down deep.

When mud turns to dust
and water holes run dry,
I'll shed my very branches
before I wither and die.

I have lived ten thousand years.
What have I to fear?
Let the world become a desert,
I will still be here!

BOBCAT WATCHING

I   thought
I was   tracking
a   bobcat.
I   was
sure   of
his   prints
in   the mud.
I felt   so smart,
so   quiet
and   sly.
Hoping   to
catch   a
glimpse   of him,
I hid   behind
a tree.   Then suddenly
I turned and   saw
him
      calmly
watching
            me.

SLOW AND STEADY

Everything I do,
I do slow and steady.
It's just the way I am.
I walk slow and steady,
about half a mile a day.
I graze slow and steady,
storing water in my shell.
I dig slow and steady,
pushing dirt before me.
I grow slow and steady,
ten years before I mate.
I evolved slow and steady,
over thousands of years!
But thanks to mankind,
my kind may disappear,
slow and steady.

HOWL

You may never see me
or even find my track.
But listen to the night.
Hear the howl of my pack.
The rancher says I steal
chickens from his pen.
But I have hungry pups
waiting in my den.
Before the rancher came
and overgrazed this land,
used up all the water
and turned soil into sand,
I lived on deer and mice.
I never had to steal.
I culled the old and sick,
and never begged a meal.
You may never see me.
But listen to my grief:
The rancher takes my land,
and then he calls me thief!

LIZARDS IN LOVE

I fell in love
in the springtime,
when the air
was cool and clean.
She was long
and low and lovely.
Her skin was
scaly and green.

I fell in love
in the springtime,
when I was foolish
and young.
It was love at first sight
when I saw her
catching ants with the tip
of her tongue!

MAGIC ROCKS

Who sat where I now sit
and drew upon this rock?
Was it a vision or some magic
that brought them here?
Could they talk to the earth
and bring down rain?
Could they heal the sick
and send away pain?
As I reach out
and touch this mystery,
I wonder:
Do they know my thoughts?
Can they sense me here?
If I close my eyes
and sit perfectly still,
will they whisper in my ear?

SHY MONSTER

I'm called a monster.
I don't know why.
I do have venom,
but I'm oh, so shy!
I chase pack rats
with my powerful legs.
I have wide jaws
to eat birds' eggs.
I mostly hunt
in morning light
before the sun
gets hot and bright.
Then under a rock
I hide away
with my chin in the dirt
for the rest of the day.

COTTONTAIL

Hit the cottontail. Behind the Over
trail bush. the limb.

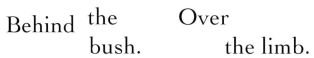

Zigzag d
o
w right.
n
left

Coyote hears you  from far off.

Owl sees you  in the dark.

 Snake smells you with his tongue.

Better
run,
little
one!

THE RATTLER

I met a cold-blooded killer
on the trail.
A chill ran down my spine.
My knees began to fail.
The sight of him shook me
to the bone.
I felt helpless
and alone.
I met a cold-blooded killer
on the trail.
And he rattled loud and clear:
Oh, please don't step on me;
I'm over here!

BE CAREFUL

Be careful when you walk
on the white sands of New Mexico,
especially in the evening
when the sun goes down,
cherry red.
Be careful
when the wind begins to blow
and sand clouds churn and rise,
silky white.
Be careful or you will tumble
with wonder and awe
into the jaws of desert light,
misty blue.
Be careful
of the mysteries you will feel,
of the secrets you will learn.
Be careful.
The person you were
may never return.

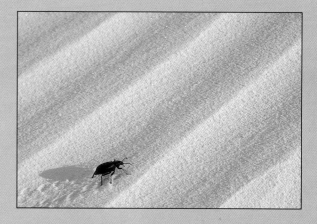

TWO RAINS

There are two rains
in the Sonoran Desert.
Like sunlight and shadow, they fall
in sharp contrast,
light and dark.
The steady, flowing rain
in November soaks the desert floor
and brings forth the owl's-clover,
primrose, and lupine of March.
But the sudden gush
of the flash flood in August
roars down the arroyo.

    It crashes and smashes and drowns
       everything in its path,
including the paloverde seed
patiently waiting for its annual bath.
The seed of this tree
needs this deadly wonder,
as does the spadefoot toad
waiting underground
for the sound of thunder.

IF I WERE AN ANT

If I were a leaf-cutter ant,
I wouldn't be a *worker* who carts leaves to the nest,
one of ten million chewers, just like all the rest.
If I were a leaf-cutter ant,
I wouldn't be a *minor* tending to the queen,
just another fungus farmer keeping things clean.
If I were a leaf-cutter ant,
I wouldn't be a *soldier* who has to guard and fight,
defending the colony all day and all night.
If I were a leaf-cutter ant,
I wouldn't be a *male* flirting and flying around,
only to fall down and die alone upon the ground.
If I were a leaf-cutter ant,
I'd be the pampered *queen*, the one and only,
supreme, royal egg-laying machine!

SAGUARO

Stand
still.
Grow
slow.
Lift
high
your arms to the sun.
Stand
still.
Grow
slow.
Lift
high
your
flowers to the sky.
Stand
still.
Grow
slow.
Hold
tight
your
water
inside.
Stand
still.
Grow
slow
and let your roots spread wide and let your roots spread wide.

HUMMINGBIRD SONG

I hear the hummingbird
as she stops to take a rest,
humming to her eggs
within her tiny nest:

I loved the way
your father flew,
so high and swift,
so sure and true.

Now he's gone.
I know not where.
But you will not
need his care.

And you will fly
as Father flew,
so high and swift,
so sure and true.

And soon enough
your day will come.
You'll leave this nest.
Your wings will hum.

When you hatch
as big as bees,
I'll feed you nectar
from flowers and trees.

ROADRUNNER

Who is the true desert bird?
Owl? Cardinal? Quail? Or sparrow?
Just wait till it gets really hot.
Just wait, and you will know.

Who is the true desert bird?
Hawk? Raven? Dove? Or wren?
Just wait till it gets really hot.
Just you wait till then.

Who is the true desert bird?
Not the ones that fly
to water holes and mountaintops
when the sun begins to fry.

Who is the true desert bird?
The one that has to stay,
the one with wings so short,
he cannot fly far away!

IF THE EARTH WERE SMALL

If the earth were small,
I'd hold it in my hands
the way a cactus holds
each drop of water.

If the earth were small,
I'd sing it a song
like the croon of a canyon wren
singing to his mate.

If the earth were small,
I'd keep it safe and sound
in a secret place, the way a pack rat
hides her treasures near her nest.

If the earth were small,
I'd keep it always in my sight
with the gaze of a great horned owl
looking down from the sky at night.

SOME NOTES ON DESERT LIFE

Breaks Free

For scientists two features distinguish deserts from all other landscapes: Rainfall is usually ten inches or less a year, and the annual amount of potential evaporation exceeds rainfall, sometimes a thousandfold. Deserts are dry, but they are not always hot. After sundown much of the day's heat radiates back into space, sometimes causing the temperature to drop more than thirty degrees at night. There are four deserts in North America: the Sonoran, the Mojave, the Great Basin, and the Chihuahuan.

LEFT PHOTO: Sand dunes. *Stovepipe Wells, Death Valley National Park, CA, March 1991*. RIGHT PHOTOS (*top to bottom*): Ocotillo in bloom. *Pinto Basin, Joshua Tree National Park, CA, April 1988*. Raven in flight. *Death Valley National Park, March 1991*.

Water Secret

Desert inhabitants have developed clever ways to obtain and maintain water. Native Americans, both ancient and modern, have sung and danced for rain. Scorpions, which kill by stinging, get water from their prey. Kangaroo rats never drink. Instead they manufacture and can survive on metabolic water. Insects lap dewdrops or sip water trapped in tiny cracks in rocks. When it rains, the roots of saguaros draw water to their trunks and arms, which have accordion-pleated ridges that allow them to "grow wide and round." A large saguaro may store several tons of water. The roots of a mesquite tree may plumb one hundred feet below the surface before they find water. Sometimes desert coyotes dig for water in the moist earth, while spadefoot toads, buried below the surface, wait for a summer thundershower to soak into the ground and wake them up.

LEFT PHOTOS (*left to right*): Saguaro and foothill paloverde. *Tucson Mountains, AZ, April 1989*. Desert star and fallen ocotillo flowers. *Pinto Basin, April 1992*. Brittlebush. *Anza-Borrego Desert State Park, CA, April 1989*. RIGHT PHOTO: Canyon tree frogs. *Romero Pools, Catalina State Park, AZ, April 1993*.

Waterless Shores

Plants are divided into two broad categories: annual and perennial. Desert annuals, such as owl's-clover and desert dandelion, cannot withstand drought—the flowers wilt and die and only the plants' seeds survive. Sometimes more than one hundred thousand seeds can be found in a square meter of shallow soil. These seeds can wait for years before the right rainfall triggers their germination. In the meantime, the seeds feed rodents, birds, and ants. Desert perennials, such as cactus, ocotillo, and paloverde, survive droughts and bloom about the same time each spring. When in bloom, annuals and perennials attract hungry and thirsty animals—from caterpillars to bighorns.

BACKGROUND PHOTO: Owl's-clover and lupine. *Ajo Mountain Drive, Organ Pipe Cactus National Monument, AZ, April 1992*. LEFT PHOTO (*inset*): Five-lined sphinx moth pollinating a desert sunflower. *Near Furnace Creek, Death Valley National Park, March 1991*. RIGHT PHOTOS (*insets, top to bottom*): Five-lined sphinx moth caterpillar eating a California poppy. *Cottonwood Basin, Joshua Tree National Park, April 1991*. Beetles on thistle. *Alamo Canyon, Organ Pipe Cactus National Monument, April 1995*.

The Oldest

The creosote bush thrives in the hottest, driest, bleakest parts of North America. In Mexico creosote is called *hediondilla*, "little stinker," because its resinous aroma fills the desert after every rain. These foul-smelling resins discourage mammals from eating the creosote. During droughts creosote bushes reduce their moisture loss by shedding first mature leaves, then baby leaves, and eventually twigs and branches. Because these survival mechanisms are so successful, creosote bushes often live a long time. Some scientists believe that one plant has been growing for more than eleven thousand years. When it sprouted, the Southwest was a mosaic of woods, grasslands, and meltwater lakes, and Ice Age mammals—like the now extinct Columbian mammoth—roamed freely.

LEFT PHOTO: Creosote bush. *Ajo Mountain Drive, April 1995.* RIGHT PHOTOS (*top to bottom*): Fossil skull of a Columbian mammoth. *Mammoth Site, Hot Springs, SD, July 1988.* Raindrop on creosote bud. *Sonoyta Valley, Organ Pipe Cactus National Monument, April 1992.*

Bobcat Watching

During the day bobcats lie on shady rock ledges, lazily surveying their domain. Like domestic cats, bobcats are curious. The stub-tailed cats will pad along rimrock silently following naturalists who study them. Bobcats are strictly carnivorous but lack the endurance of coyotes or foxes, which chase their prey. At night bobcats stalk within a few feet of their prey, then spring out of the shadows. Adult bobcats are solitary, except for a two-day courtship each year. Kittens are born in March or April, two or three to a litter, and stay with their mothers into the fall to learn the art of being sly.

LEFT PHOTOS (*top to bottom*): Bobcat sleeping. *April 1990.* Bobcat resting. *April 1989.* RIGHT PHOTO: Bobcat watching. *April 1989.* All photos: *Arizona-Sonora Desert Museum, Tucson, AZ.*

Slow and Steady

Desert tortoises may live for more than one hundred years. To escape the heat in summer and the cold in winter, tortoises retreat to their burrows. During the early spring, tortoises eat juicy wildflowers. Water from these flowers is stored in the tortoise's canteen-like bladder. After the summer thundershowers, tortoises replenish their bladders by drinking rainwater. Tortoises have had trouble in the twentieth century. As more people visit the desert, more tortoises are taken away as pets or killed during motorcycle races.

LEFT PHOTO: Desert tortoise. *Pinto Mountains, Joshua Tree National Park, March 1988.* RIGHT PHOTOS (*left to right*): Desert tortoise eating beaver tail cactus pad. *Pinto Mountains, March 1988.* Tracks of desert tortoise across sand dune. *Pinto Basin, March 1988.*

Howl

Desert coyotes weigh about twenty pounds, half the size of their mountain cousins. In the desert smaller animals have an advantage because they radiate heat more easily than larger animals and therefore need to drink less water. Desert coyotes' pale, thin fur radiates heat better than the dark, thick, and insulating fur of their mountain-bound relatives. Although they eat a wide variety of plants and animals, coyotes eat so many gophers, ground squirrels, and mice that they help to keep the desert from becoming overrun with rodents. Adult coyotes and their offspring form the nucleus of the celebrated and noisy pack. Some scientists believe the coyotes' staccato howls audibly mark the pack's territory; others believe they help locate missing family members, prepare the pack for a hunt, or simply broadcast the animals' exuberance.

BACKGROUND PHOTO: Valley between the Ajo and the Diablo Mountains. *Organ Pipe Cactus National Monument, April 1996.* LEFT PHOTO (*inset*): Coyote resting. *The Living Desert, Palm Desert, CA, March 1988.* RIGHT PHOTO (*inset*): Coyote howling. *The Living Desert, March 1988.*

Lizards in Love

As a group, lizards do well in heat. In the Mojave a healthy desert iguana was found to have a body temperature of 118 degrees Fahrenheit. To conserve their bodily water, lizards excrete their metabolic wastes as semisolid uric acid instead of as urine. Lizards are strange and animated creatures. When frightened, collared lizards run upright on their hind legs like tiny dinosaurs. If handled roughly or startled, horned lizards squirt blood from their eyes. Male collared lizards do "push-ups" to attract mates.

LEFT PHOTO: Collared lizard. *Sabino Canyon, Tucson, AZ, April 1990.* RIGHT PHOTOS (*top to bottom*): Regal horned lizard. *Arizona-Sonora Desert Museum, April 1990.* Desert iguana. *The Living Desert, March 1988.*

Magic Rocks

Petroglyphs are symbols that have been pecked or scratched in rock by people from prehistoric cultures. They are found throughout the Southwest and some are more than a thousand years old. Petroglyph styles and symbols differ by region and time period. Therefore one symbol may have multiple meanings. Some petroglyphs may have been made to mark a territory or a trail, to aid hunting or fertility, to contact the gods, or to tell a story. The spiral, a very common petroglyph symbol, was used by the Hopi people when a settlement was deserted.

LEFT PHOTOS (*top to bottom*): Bighorn petroglyph. *Three Rivers Petroglyph Site, Tularosa Basin, NM, April 1996.* Signal Hill. *Saguaro National Park, AZ, April 1990.* RIGHT PHOTOS (*top to bottom*): Geometric design. *Three Rivers Petroglyph Site, April 1996.* Raven petroglyph. *Three Rivers Petroglyph Site, April 1996.*

Shy Monster

Gila monsters are rarely seen residents of Arizona and Sonora, Mexico. They occasionally range into Utah, New Mexico, Nevada, and California. Gila monsters have excellent daytime vision and acute hearing. Within the United States, Gila monsters are the only lizards with forked tongues and the only venomous lizards. Because Gila monsters eat defenseless prey— baby rodents, reptile and bird eggs, and nestlings— which are easy to subdue without venom, most biologists believe Gila monsters' venom is intended to threaten the lizards' predators, like coyotes and kit foxes. Their venom is not fatal to humans. Gila monsters convert excess food to fat, which is stored in their tails. A fat tail is the sign of a well-fed lizard, and a thin tail means food has been scarce.

LEFT PHOTOS (*top to bottom*): Gila monster. *Tucson Mountains, April 1996.* Pack rat. *Arizona-Sonora Desert Museum, April 1996.* RIGHT PHOTO: Gila monster in an arroyo. *Tucson Mountains, April 1996.*

Cottontail

Cottontails are agile and speedy. However, their survival as a species depends on prolific breeding, for they are hunted by formidable predators. Coyotes often hunt in pairs, chasing the rabbit in turns until it tires. Snakes mostly smell with their tongues. Odor particles stick to the tip of a snake's forked tongue. These prongs transfer scent particles to tiny holes on the roof of the snake's mouth, called the Jacobson's organ, which reads the odors. On moonless nights, when narrow desert canyons are as dark as mine shafts, owls see clearly because their eyes are sensitive to dim light. Owls' ears are positioned at different heights on each side of the head, helping owls pinpoint cottontails across a seemingly noiseless desert.

LEFT PHOTOS (*top to bottom*): Desert cottontail. *Pinto Mountains, March 1988.* Coyote running. *The Living Desert, March 1989.* RIGHT PHOTOS (*clockwise from left*): Western rattlesnake. *Near Rapid City, SD, July 1988.* Long-eared owl in fan palm. *Cottonwood Springs, Joshua Tree National Park, March 1988.* Desert cottontail grooming. *Sabino Canyon, April 1990.*

The Rattler

Rattlesnakes are truly North American reptiles. They evolved on the desert plains of Mexico between four and twelve million years ago and then spread throughout the warm and temperate regions of the continent. (One species reached the northern parts of South America.) There are eleven species of rattlesnakes in Arizona alone. Each one prefers different habitats and foods, although all are carnivorous. Most scientists believe that rattlesnakes developed loosely attached keratin rattles to amplify the vibrating sound of their tails, which helps them avoid being stepped on. The warning buzz usually works. Most people bitten by rattlesnakes are either handling or attacking them.

LEFT PHOTO: Western diamondback rattlesnake. *Tucson Mountains, April 1993.* RIGHT PHOTO: Western rattlesnake. *Near Rapid City, SD, July 1988.*

Be Careful

Most of the world's sand is eroded quartz. But there are other kinds of sand, too. The white sand dunes of the Chihuahuan Desert, which cover more than three hundred square miles of southern New Mexico, are nearly pure gypsum, a mineral as fine and white as sugar. Sand dunes change shape, grain by grain, whenever the wind blows. During storms at White Sands, dust rises and often causes temporary whiteouts as the boundary between earth and sky dissolves into clouds of gypsum. Because of the unusual collection of plants that grow there, some biologists consider White Sands to be a desert within a desert.

BACKGROUND PHOTO: Sandstorm. *White Sands National Monument, NM, April 1996.* LEFT PHOTO (*inset*): Soap tree yuccas. *White Sands National Monument, April 1996.* RIGHT PHOTO (*inset*): Darkling beetle or stinkbug walking across sand. *White Sands National Monument, April 1996.*

Two Rains

The Arizona portion of the Sonoran Desert has two rainy seasons, making it the greenest desert in North America. The gentle winter rains penetrate the ground and awaken the seeds of the annual wildflowers. The heavy, soaking summer thundershowers send torrents of water rushing down arroyos, flinging paloverde and other seeds against tumbling stones, which causes their coats to crack open so germination may begin. Animals depend on the rain cycles, too. Red-spotted toads breed in the spring, when rainwater fills pools along an arroyo or seeps up from the ground in a shaded canyon. As the desert heats up, the toads absorb water from the damp ground through a thin patch of belly skin. Spadefoot toads, which breed in the summer, are awakened from their subterranean retreats by the sound of the summer thundershowers.

LEFT PHOTO: Blue paloverde. *Saguaro National Park, April 1990.* RIGHT PHOTOS (*clockwise from top left*): Desert paintbrush. *San Pedro River Valley, AZ, March 1992.* Arroyo with water. *Saguaro National Park, April 1993.* Red-spotted toad in breeding pool. *Cottonwood Springs, March 1988.*

If I Were an Ant

Leaf-cutter ants are underground fungus farmers. Workers gather leaves, flowers, and buds outside their colony then bring them underground to other workers who chew them up and fertilize them with their own feces. From this concoction grows a special fungus, the ants' only source of food. Big-headed soldier ants protect the colony from predatory ants and lizards. But the survival of each colony rests with the queen, who is fed and groomed by tiny minor ants below the ground in a special egg-laying chamber.

BOTH PHOTOS: Mexican leaf-cutter ants carrying a petal (*left*) and buds (*right*) of the blue paloverde down a tree trunk. *Organ Pipe Cactus National Monument, April 1995.*

Saguaro

Most people think of saguaros (pronounced *sa-WHAR-os*) as the symbol of all North American deserts, but they actually grow only in a restricted portion of the Sonoran Desert. Saguaros may grow more than fifty feet tall, have more than thirty arms, and live for almost two hundred years. They are the source of both food and shelter for many desert animals. Bats and birds feed on the nectar of the waxy white flowers. Coyotes and rodents eat the sweet red fruit. Woodpeckers excavate nest cavities in the trunks and arms. When abandoned, these cavities shelter owls. Even a fallen, rotting saguaro may protect lizards or snakes.

LEFT PHOTO: Saguaros and blooming brittlebush. *Sabino Canyon, April 1992.* RIGHT PHOTOS (*left to right*): Curve-billed thrasher pollinating a saguaro flower. *Sabino Canyon, April 1990.* White-winged dove perched on a saguaro. *Tucson Mountains, April 1992.*

Hummingbird Song

Hummingbirds need plenty of energy, as they lose a large portion their body weight during hot desert days. Their hearts may beat twelve hundred times a minute as they fly forward or backward or hover. Hummingbirds can reach speeds of up to forty-five miles per hour and often migrate long distances. During courtship, some males dazzle their prospective mates with pendulum-like aerial displays. After mating, the male leaves to search for another mate, leaving nest building, incubation, and chick rearing to the female. To obtain energy, hummingbirds drink nectar. Spiders and insects gleaned from flowers or caught in the air provide hummingbirds with protein, which is particularly essential for growing chicks.

LEFT PHOTO: Female black-chinned hummingbird incubating eggs. *Sonoyta Valley, April 1995.* RIGHT PHOTO: Male black-chinned hummingbird feeding. *Arizona-Sonora Desert Museum, April 1993.*

Roadrunner

Roadrunners range from the Pacific coast of California to the humid woods of Louisiana and across the southern plains. Yet they thrive in all North American deserts. Most birds use body fluids to flush excess salts through their urinary tracks, but roadrunners have a gland in their nose that concentrates and eliminates salt crystals. While roadrunners are notorious for eating rattlesnakes, they more frequently eat insects, scorpions, baby birds, and lizards. In fact, unlike most other birds, roadrunners hunt in the heat of the day when lizards are active. On cold winter days, roadrunners bask in the sun. The black skin on their backs, revealed when they part their feathers, absorbs the sun's energy. This allows roadrunners to keep warm without having to constantly search for food.

LEFT PHOTOS (*clockwise from top left*): Raven. *Near Furnace Creek, March 1991.* Gambel quail. *Sonoyta Valley, April 1995.* Red-tailed hawk on a saguaro. *Valley of the Ajo, April 1995.* Mourning dove. *Catalina State Park, April 1993.* RIGHT PHOTOS (*left to right*): Male cardinal in mesquite. *Sabino Canyon, April 1992.* Roadrunner with a whiptail lizard. *Catalina State Park, April 1993.*

If the Earth Were Small

The desert is raw and majestic, a land reduced to essentials. The earth is a thousand shades of brown, highlighted by bursts of color. So clean is the air, so busy the wind, that one writer imagined the desert to be "the lungs" of North America. From mountain rim to mountain rim across scorching plains, the desert may seem desolate, but it is far from deserted.

LEFT PHOTO: View of the Roskruge Mountains across the Avra Valley. *Signal Hill, AZ, April 1992.* RIGHT PHOTOS (*top to bottom*): Great horned owl. *The Living Desert, March 1988.* Joshua trees at sunset. *Lost Horse Valley, Joshua Tree National Park, April 1989.*